Ride Faster

A Story of Israel Barlow

Written by

The Barlow Family

Illustrated by

Mousam Banerjee

Come, said Grandpa Barlow. Sit near me by the fire. I want to tell you an important story of a time when I was asked to deliver a message for the Prophet.

I had delivered many messages for him before, but this particular message was going to a family living in a neighborhood where folks were hostile to the Saints.

Before I left with the message, Brother Joseph warned me, "Let them put your horse up for you and accept their invitation to eat supper with them. But when it is sundown, saddle your horse and leave.

They will be insistent and try to persuade you to remain overnight. But if you value your life, do not stay, but leave, and listen to the direction of the Spirit."

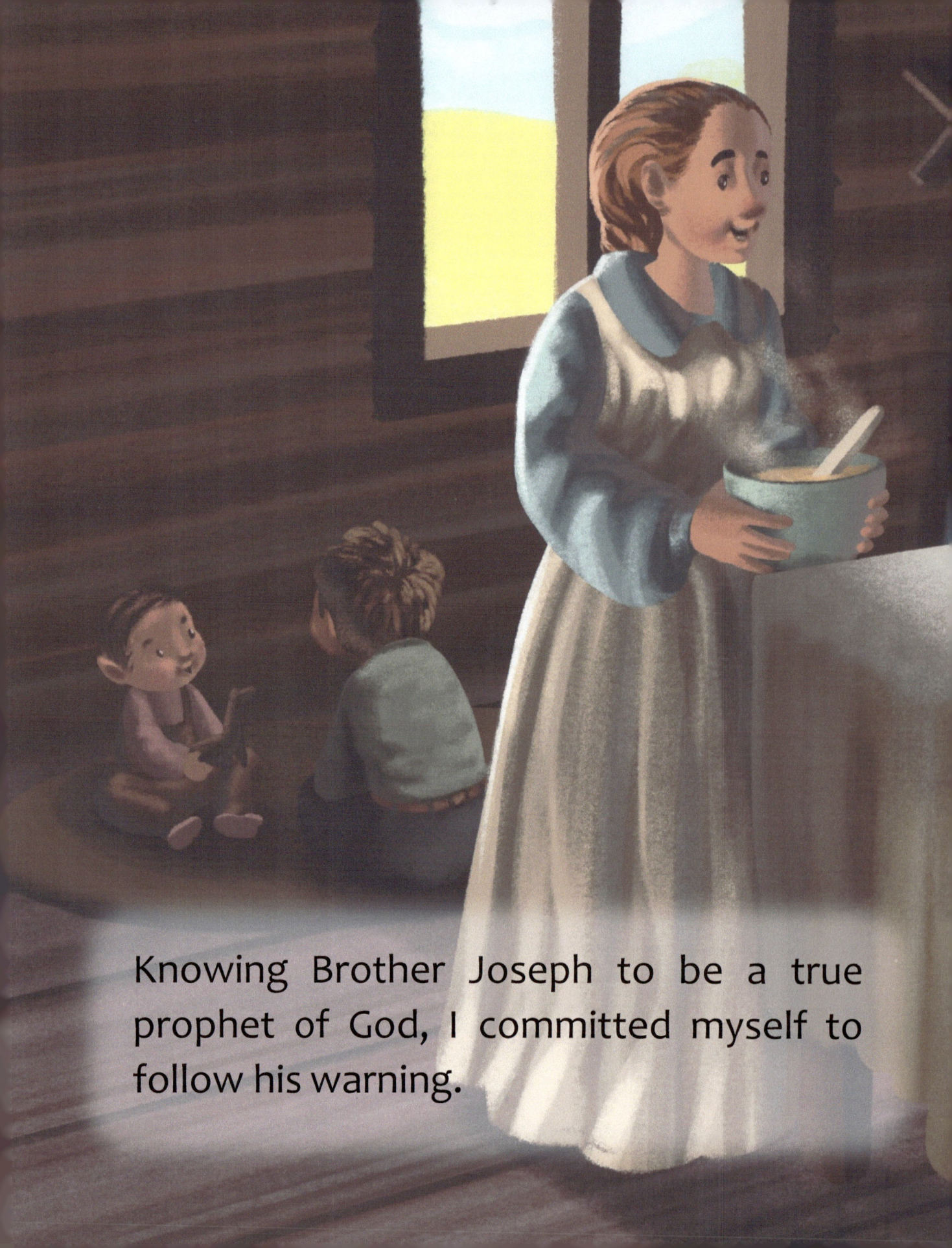

Knowing Brother Joseph to be a true prophet of God, I committed myself to follow his warning.

I delivered the message without problem.
Just as the prophet foresaw, the family
invited me to eat and was very hospitable.

As the evening neared, I went to ready my horse. "Stay," they insisted—reminding me of the long journey ahead.

I thanked them for their kindness, but mounted my horse, and promptly started back to Nauvoo at sundown.

I rode peacefully along the country road until it became dark. Suddenly a voice said, "Ride faster".

I sat up in the saddle and looked around. Though I did not see anything that would require my haste, I nudged my horse faster.

As I rounded a bend and approached a bridge, I heard the voice repeat, "Ride faster!" Recognizing the Spirit, I urged my horse to a gallop.

"Ride for your life!" the Spirit suddenly commanded. I spurred my horse on, racing through the darkness.

As I thundered over the bridge, I heard a mob yelling and cursing. As they scrambled to mount their horses they shouted, "He's getting away!"

A short distance down the path, the Spirit commanded, "Turn to the right". I slowed my horse and turned sharply to the right and off the road.

I stood in silence as a wave of pounding hooves raced past me down the road.

As the sound of horses and angry men faded, I made my way to the river's edge before backtracking away from the mob.

Exhausted but grateful to be alive, I traveled all night across the countryside to arrive at Nauvoo. I knew that obeying the prophet and listening to the Spirit had saved my life.

As I entered Nauvoo, the sun was beginning to rise. I could see Brother Joseph pacing outside his home.

Joseph looked up as I approached, relief in his eyes. He'd been up all night. I started to tell him what had happened— the voice, the mob that had been waiting—but he stopped me.

"I saw it all," he said. "You have no need to tell me." Then placing his hand on my shoulder he gave me a blessing, "Israel, thee and thine shall never want."

"That blessing applies to all of you," Grandpa Barlow explained. "But even greater blessings come from following the prophet and the Spirit. Following the prophet and Spirit may save your life and will lead you to eternal life."

The Life of Israel Barlow

Israel Barlow was born in Granville, Massachusetts to Jonathan Barlow and Annis Gillett, on September 13, 1806. Israel was the oldest surviving child and from an early age had to work hard as a farmer, with lumber, as a nurseryman, a wheelwright, horticulturist, and rancher.

Israel tells about his spiritual yearnings as a child. His parents had taught him what was right and what was wrong. He then felt impressed to teach his playmates the difference between right and wrong. He taught them to pray to prepare them to live a good life, so that they might go to heaven. From this early age he found that he possessed a natural ability and a great desire to preach.

At about the age of 12, Israel started accompanying his father to New York while he looked for a place to settle. They chose some land in Canandaigua, New York, near his uncle Abner Barlow. The whole family moved there by 1820 when Israel's father suddenly passed away. Israel was only fourteen. Israel's mother remarried and had two more children when her second husband suddenly passed away. Shortly after his death the family moved to the nearby town of Mendon, New York. Their good friends and neighbors included Brigham Young, his wife, parents and siblings and their families, as well as Heber C. Kimball and Vilate, his wife. Israel was baptized in Mendon, New York by Brigham Young on May 16, 1832. Eventually his mother and all his siblings joined as well.

Israel and his mother and family traveled to Ohio where he was invited to join Zion's Camp. Zion's Camp included 205 men who marched to Missouri and back to Ohio led by the Prophet Joseph Smith. Some of his duties were to care for horses and to cook with Joseph Young. He and Joseph Young arose each morning at 3 a.m. to prepare breakfast and retired each night after midnight. Israel cherished his experiences with Zion's Camp since it gave him so many opportunities to be close to and learn from the Prophet. From among the 205 men of that journey, the Lord called his church leaders, including Israel who was ordained into the First Quorum of the Seventy on January 30, 1835.

After helping work on building Kirtland and the Kirtland Temple, Israel and his family traveled to Missouri where they were persecuted again. Israel and 31 others were advised by Brigham Young to depart from Far West in October to help find a place for the 12,000 displaced Saints to settle. Israel was part of a committee of three who looked for a suitable place. Mr. Galland was willing to sell the land then known as Commerce, Illinois. The location was approved by Joseph Smith, who was in jail in Missouri. The land was purchased and improved to become the city of Nauvoo.

While displaced in Quincy, Illinois, Israel met and married Elizabeth Haven. Elizabeth and Israel were married on February 23, 1840 in Quincy, by Isaac Morley. From there they moved to Nauvoo. While in Nauvoo four children were born to them. Their oldest son, James Nathaniel, was born and died on May 8, 1841. Years later while traveling through Nauvoo on a mission to England, Elizabeth asked Israel to find little James' grave and rebury him in the main cemetery. Israel wrote to Elizabeth, telling about his experience of finding little James' grave and reburying him.

When Brigham Young departed from Nauvoo in 1846, he instructed Israel Barlow and Joseph Young to remain behind. Their duties were to help the Saints cross the Mississippi River; care for the unfortunate who were unable to go; look after Nauvoo property and dispose of what they could not sell before they left. While waiting to leave Nauvoo, Elizabeth gave birth to their fourth child on May 1, 1846. Finally, the family departed Nauvoo taking with them two orphan children, and Aunt Betsy.

Israel and Elizabeth traveled across Iowa where Israel helped construct seven hundred homes and dugouts that made up Winter Quarters. Israel and his family lived in a log house while they stayed and farmed due to lack of supplies. Israel and Elizabeth were in attendance on December 27, 1847, when Brigham Young was sustained as the President of the Church. Finally, Israel and his family prepared to leave Winter Quarters and travel with Brigham Young's company of 1848. They arrived in the Salt Lake Valley on September 23, 1848.

Israel picked out 160 acres to farm in Bountiful. Israel discovered that the land in Bountiful was especially rich and he was able to not only harvest grains but raised abundant fruits and vegetables. For years he traveled to Salt Lake City to sell his produce. He was a noted horticulturist and could graft multiple fruits on the same tree. Brigham Young and other close friends and associates would often travel to Bountiful to enjoy fresh watermelon at Israel Barlow's place.

Four and a half years after arriving in the Valley Israel received a call at General Conference, April 8, 1853, to serve a mission in England. While on the journey a severe storm threatened the ship. The captain declared that the ship was going to sink. Israel and the other elders went into their room and prayed for safety. The sea calmed and the elders could see six angels guarding the ship, two of whom were recognized as Joseph and Hyrum Smith. Upon arrival Israel was assigned to take charge of the Birmingham and Warwickshire Conferences where he worked for most of his mission. In 1855 he was asked to take charge of a group of saints gathering to Utah. He brought 581 saints from Liverpool, England. Among this group was a young woman by the name of Lucy Heap. Israel arrived back in the Valley on September 24, 1855 with a large group of immigrants. On December 2, 1855, Israel and 19-year-old Lucy Heap were married, with the permission of his other wives and of the church authorities. The authors are descended from Israel and Lucy's first child, Truman Heap.

Israel worked hard to reestablish the farm in Bountiful that had been neglected by a renter. Because of the renter's great neglect, Elizabeth and the family had suffered greatly. Israel upon his return continued in his calling as the President of the Sixth Quorum of the Seventy. Their meetings' notes describe Israel's devotion to the Lord, and his wisdom in leading the Quorum. In 1882 Israel was released as President of the Sixth Quorum of the Seventy and ordained a patriarch by Wilford Woodruff on December 8, 1882.

Israel's final days were very trying. He was confined to bed with consumption, or tuberculosis of the lungs, which he had contracted while in England thirty years before. He died November 1, 1883 at the age of 77.

Information taken from "The Israel Barlow Story and Mormon Mores" by Ora Haven Barlow

www.ingramcontent.com/pod-product-compliance
Lightning Source LLC
Chambersburg PA
CBHW042014090426
42811CB00015B/1647